Island ENERGY

THE SUPERHERO ENERGIES THAT POWER THE CARIBBEAN

WRITTEN BY
ZOLA HINDS

ILLUSTRATIONS BY
KABRENA L. ROBINSON

WEST INDIES

Island Energy
Text copyright © 2024 by Zola Hinds
Illustration copyright © 2024 by Kabrena L. Robinson

First Edition 2024

ISBN
Paperback 978-1-998245-09-3

Book design by Kabrena L. Robinson
Published by Eva-Michelle & Family Publishing
www.evamichelleandfamily.com

I dedicate this book to the little girl within with big dreams and to the souls who lent their hands in helping her craft those dreams into reality.

-Z.H.

Let's journey to the sweet, tropical Caribbean
to discover the amazing world of energy.

The golden sunshine.
The nice warm tropical breeze.

The winding rivers, the luscious forests,
and the high mountain peaks
are all part of the many ways
we can power the islands using sustainable energy.

Solar Energy

Imagine the sun like a giant, glowing superhero in the sky, giving us light and warmth every day.

In the Caribbean, we have lots of sunny days, which makes it perfect for using solar panels.

Solar panels work by capturing sunlight and turning it into electricity. They use special materials called photovoltaic cells to convert the rays from the golden sun into usable energy, bringing electricity to homes, schools, and even beachside smoothie stands.

So, when you see those shiny panels on rooftops or in open fields, remember they are like the sun's helpers, working hard to make sure we have the energy to play, learn, and do all the fun things we love.

Wind Energy

Wind energy is like an invisible superhero that can spin giant, tall towers called wind turbines.

These turbines have big, twirling blades that catch the wind's energy and turn it into electricity.

The **cool Caribbean winds** can be harnessed to create **wind power,**

turning breezy days into energy-packed beats that keep the lights on and the music playing.

Wind power helps to light up our homes, power our gadgets, and create clean energy for our islands.

Hydroelectric Energy

Hydroelectric energy is the water superhero that helps us create electricity.

Imagine a big, powerful wheel called a water turbine. When water rushes through it, the wheel spins. That spinning energy is turned into electricity!

Smart engineers build special dams and water channels to guide the water and create a splashy dance that turns into electricity.

These dams and reservoirs also help to prevent flooding and provide our homes with clean drinking water and irrigation systems for our farmlands

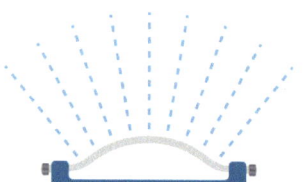

So, when you see those water wheels or hear the rush of a waterfall, know that they're working hard to give us the energy we need for our everyday lives.

Geothermal Energy

Geothermal energy is the superhero that gives
us warm hugs from the Earth deep below.

Imagine hot springs bubbling up or steam
coming out of the ground.
This heat from the earth's underground can be
transformed into electricity.

Skilful engineers dig deep wells into the Earth, to find that warm, toasty energy. This **heat** is then turned into **steam** that powers turbines to create **electricity**!

This electricity can be used to keep our homes nice and cool on those hot sunny days.

The Eastern Caribbean is a hotbed of volcanic activity. These fiery islands are perfect for harnessing the power of geothermal energy to create electricity.

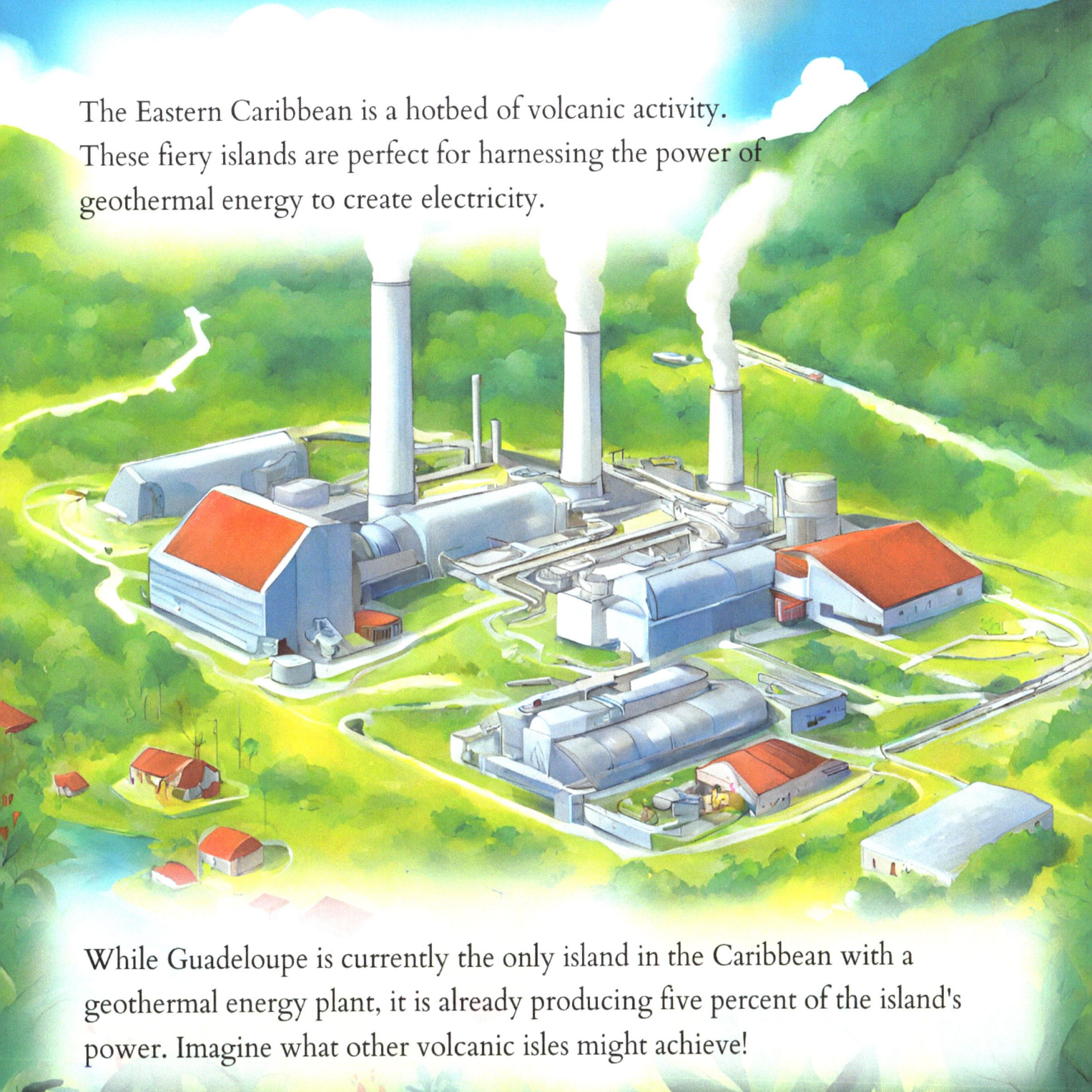

While Guadeloupe is currently the only island in the Caribbean with a geothermal energy plant, it is already producing five percent of the island's power. Imagine what other volcanic isles might achieve!

Nuclear Energy

Nuclear energy is like having a tiny army of atom superheroes that can make a lot of electricity.

Picture it like a super battery that can last a really long time.

Clever scientists use a special process called Nuclear Fission, where they split these tiny atoms apart, and when that happens, lots of energy is released.

Strong miners dig up rocks with Uranium from the earth.

This is carried to a place called a **Power Station** and put into a big machine called a **Nuclear Reactor**. This controls how fast the tiny atoms in the Uranium break apart to make just the right amount of heat.

POWER STATION

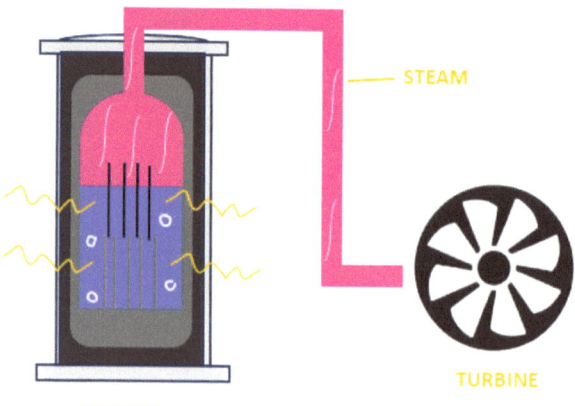

STEAM

REACTOR

TURBINE

GENERATOR

This heat boils water, making steam. The steam spins a big fan called a **Turbine**, creating electricity. This electricity can travel through cables to give light to many homes.

Smart scientists in Jamaica are carefully planning and researching ways to harness nuclear energy for generating electricity to power homes, schools, hospitals, and even your favourite games and gadgets.

All of these energy sources keep our islands up and running and help us in our daily lives.

Our islands' energy comes in many forms, each with its unique rhythm and melody that makes the world we live in safer, cleaner, and more sustainable for all.

About the Author

Zola Hinds

Zola Hinds was born and brought up in Jamaica. She currently resides in the UK as a PhD student in Nuclear Engineering after completing a Master's as a British Council Women in STEM Scholar at Bangor University in 2021.

Her experience as a Climate Advocate includes participation in the Girls Climate Action for Resilience & Empowerment (GirlsCARE) program. Additionally, she has served as Director of Project Planning for the Jamaica Climate Change Youth Council, spearheading the Albion Heights project, an initiative funded by the UNDP to mitigate the impact of Climate Change and create a 'Green Community'. The project included the installation of renewable energy solar panels, rainwater harvesting, and community recycling systems in ten households.

Zola's inspiration for this book was fuelled by curiosity and the scarcity of information on 'nuclear energy in the Caribbean'. She decided to bridge the gap by creating a children's book that simplifies the complexities of nuclear energy and other regional energy sources while weaving in elements of Caribbean culture and inclusivity.

In her spare time, Zola enjoys going to the beach, dancing, and eating Jamaican food.

Sources

 https://www.nnl.co.uk/employee-area/cop26/nuclear-energy-a-kids-guide/

 https://www.carilec.org

 https://www.nrel.gov

 https://www.energy.gov